HOI!

HELLO, ...!

your name here

WELCOME TO **AMSTERDAM,**
THE CITY OF BRIDGES, CANALS, AND BIKES!
READY TO DISCOVER MORE?
TURN THE PAGE TO START YOUR ADVENTURE!

TO ISAAC AND AARON,
THE MOST CURIOUS AND ADVENTUROUS KIDS I KNOW
– MAMMA –

The ABCs of Amsterdam: a first guide to the capital
of the Netherlands by Paola Bucciol.
Published by City ABC Books.
© 2021 Paola Bucciol
No portion of this book may be reproduced in any form
without permission from the publisher.
For permissions, visit: www.cityabcbooks.com
ISBN: 978-90-831817-4-5
Cover design and illustrations by Anca Ioana Boștină.
Graphic design by Aluycia Suceng.
First Edition

THE
ABCs
OF
AMSTERDAM

A FIRST GUIDE TO THE CAPITAL OF THE NETHERLANDS

Can you find all of
the 20 Dutch flags
hidden throughout
the book?

WRITTEN BY PAOLA BUCCIOL

illustrated by Anca Ioana Boștină

This is the *Magere Brug*.
Most bridges over the Amstel open
to let tall ships pass.

There are
more than
1,200 bridges
in Amsterdam!

A is for AMSTEL RIVER

THE CITY OF AMSTERDAM IS NAMED AFTER THIS RIVER.
AMSTERDAM MEANS "DAM ON THE AMSTEL".

Bakfiets *(bucket bike)*
In the past, these special bikes were used to carry goods. Today, the bucket is a fun and safe way to transport kids.

B

is for BIKES
(in Dutch: *fietsen*)

BIKING IS A FAST, SAFE, AND FUN WAY TO GET AROUND AMSTERDAM. EVERYONE RIDES A BIKE IN THIS CITY!

Barge

Rental boat, a great
way to explore the city

Boats come
in all shapes
and sizes!

Tour boat

C
is for CANALS
(in Dutch: *grachten*)

CANALS ARE AMSTERDAM'S WATERWAYS.
THEY ARE BUSTLING WITH BOATS OF
ALL KINDS—FROM BARGES TRANSPORTING
GOODS, TO PADDLE BOATS, TO TOUR BOATS
TAKING VISITORS AROUND THE CITY.

is for D
DAM SQUARE
(locally known as "*De Dam*")

On Sundays from mid-Spring to mid-Fall, kids of all ages gather around the puppet theater in front of the Palace.

THE DAM IS THE SITE OF THE ROYAL PALACE. THE ROYAL FAMILY DOESN'T LIVE IN THIS PALACE, BUT OFFICIAL RECEPTIONS AND ROYAL EVENTS ARE OFTEN HELD IN ITS GRAND HALLS.

E is for EETCAFÉ
(Dutch word for diner)

Some diners only serve pancakes. Do you know that the Dutch have their own pancake style? *Pannenkoeken* are thin and large pancakes eaten for lunch or dinner.

KIDS WELCOME!

EETCAFÉS ARE A GREAT STOP FOR *BROODJES* (SANDWICHES) OR *APPELTAART* (APPLE PIE). MANY DINERS HAVE CRAYONS AND COLORING PAGES FOR KIDS, AND EVEN COZY CORNERS WITH BOOKS AND TOYS. *EET SMAKELIJK* (ENJOY YOUR MEAL) AND HAVE FUN!

Anne wanted to be a writer and planned to turn her diary into a book. She never finished her project because she didn't survive the war. But, her dad found and published her diary after the war, making Anne's dream come true.

Like many other Jewish people, the Franks went into hiding to save their lives. The house where they hid—and Anne wrote her diary—is now a museum dedicated to Anne's life story.

is for ANNE FRANK
(1929-1945)

ANNE WAS A JEWISH GIRL WHO LIVED IN AMSTERDAM DURING WORLD WAR II. HER WARTIME DIARY KEEPS INSPIRING READERS OF ALL AGES BECAUSE, DESPITE THE GREAT DANGERS SHE AND OTHER JEWISH PEOPLE FACED AT THAT TIME, IT IS FILLED WITH DREAMS , LOVE FOR LIFE, AND HOPE.

G is for GEZELLIG

(untranslatable Dutch word, similar to cozy, pronounced heh-SELL-ick)

What things do you think are *gezellig?*

FROM PLAYDATES TO SNUGGLES AND CUDDLES, *GEZELLIG* IS EVERYTHING THAT MAKES YOU FEEL COZY AND HAPPY WITH YOUR LOVED ONES.

Moored boats and barges provide additional bike parking lots, extra outdoor cafe seating, and even space for fully-equipped playgrounds.

HOUSEBOATS ARE COMFORTABLE HOMES ON WATER. THEY ARE PERMANENTLY ANCHORED (OR MOORED), SO THEY DON'T MOVE. THERE ARE 2,500 HOUSEBOATS IN THE CANALS OF AMSTERDAM!

is for HOUSEBOATS
(in Dutch: *woonboten*)

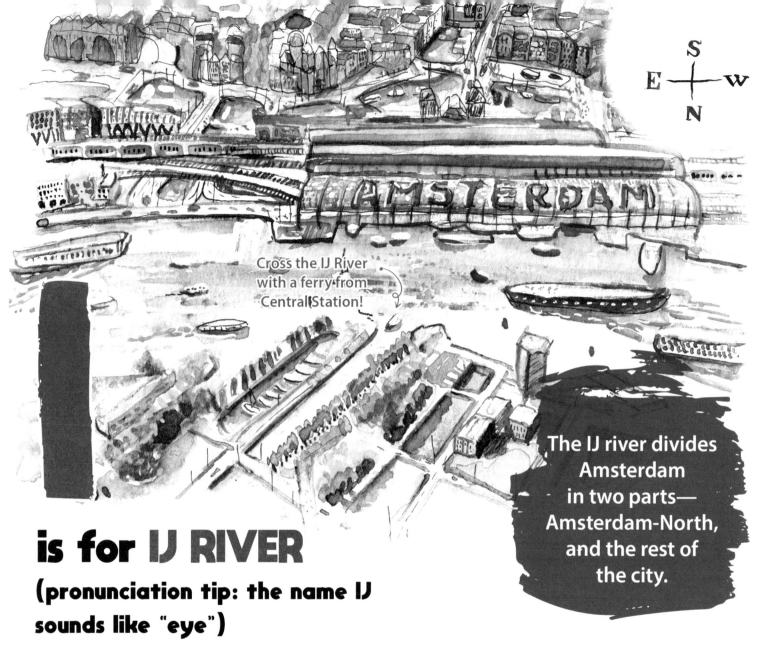

Cross the IJ River with a ferry from Central Station!

The IJ river divides Amsterdam in two parts— Amsterdam-North, and the rest of the city.

is for IJ RIVER

(pronunciation tip: the name IJ sounds like "eye")

THIS RIVER IS AMSTERDAM'S BUSIEST WATERWAY, WITH HUNDREDS OF BARGES, SHIPS, AND FERRIES TRAVELING OVER IT EVERYDAY.
IJ IS A ONE-LETTER NAME—I AND J TOGETHER FORM A LETTER UNIQUE TO THE DUTCH ALPHABET!

Until 200 years ago, buildings in Amsterdam didn't have street numbers. Instead, many homes and businesses had *gevelstenen*, decorated bricks with landmarks that people could remember.

is for JORDAAN

(pronunciation tip: "J" in Dutch sounds like "y" in "yard")

AMSTERDAM'S JORDAAN NEIGHBORHOOD IS KNOWN FOR ITS BEAUTIFUL OLD AND CROOKED HOUSES.

K is for KINGDOM

THE NETHERLANDS ARE A KINGDOM. THAT MEANS THEY HAVE A KING AND QUEEN. WILLEM-ALEXANDER OF ORANGE AND HIS WIFE MÁXIMA ARE THE KING AND QUEEN OF THE NETHERLANDS.

Do you know why Dutch national sport teams wear orange uniforms? Orange is the traditional Dutch color, in honor of the Royal Family, the House of Oranje-Nassau. Dutch people wear orange on national celebrations!

STROOPWAFELS

FRIET MET MAYO

HARING

Try these snacks when you stroll at any daily market around the city!

is for LEKKER!

(Dutch word for yummy, nice, good, pleasant)

YOU WILL HEAR THIS WORD MOSTLY WHEN TALKING ABOUT FOOD, BUT YOU CAN SAY "*LEKKER*" JUST ABOUT ANYTHING THAT MAKES YOU THINK "I LIKE THIS!"

POFFERTJES

is for
MUSEUMS

AMSTERDAM HAS MORE
THAN 100 MUSEUMS!
THEY COVER JUST ABOUT
ANYTHING—THE CITY'S
HISTORY, SCIENCE, ART,
MARITIME HISTORY,
MOVIES, EVEN MICROBES!

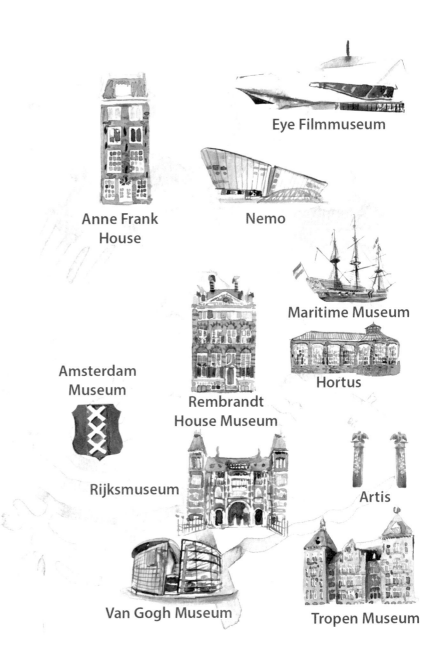

Anne Frank
House

Eye Filmmuseum

Nemo

Maritime Museum

Amsterdam
Museum

Rembrandt
House Museum

Hortus

Rijksmuseum

Artis

Van Gogh Museum

Tropen Museum

is for NETHERLANDS N

NETHERLANDS MEANS "LOW-LYING LANDS" BECAUSE PART OF THE COUNTRY IS BELOW SEA LEVEL. THROUGHOUT HISTORY, THE DUTCH HAVE BUILT SPECIAL BARRIERS CALLED *DIJKEN* (DIKES) TO PROTECT THEIR LAND FROM FLOODING.

If a street name ends in "dijk", it means that that street was originally (and sometimes still is) a dike.

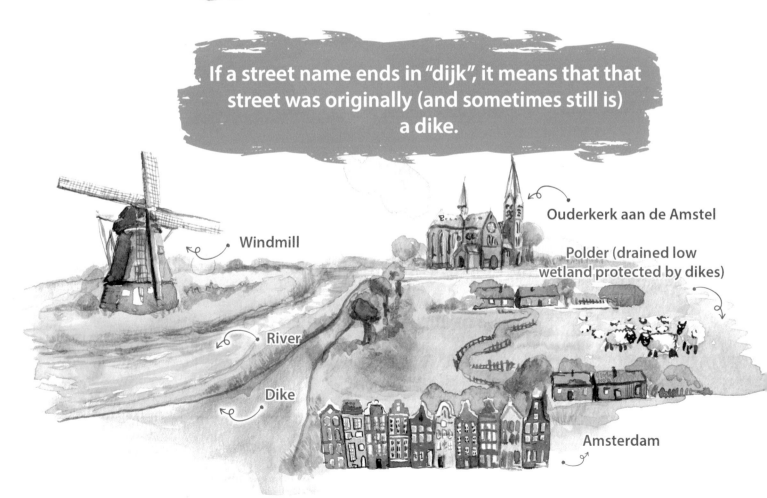

Windmill

River

Dike

Ouderkerk aan de Amstel

Polder (drained low wetland protected by dikes)

Amsterdam

O is for OLIEBOLLEN
(Dutch-style dough balls)

THESE COLD-SEASON TREATS ARE PLAIN OR FILLED WITH RAISINS, AND SPRINKLED WITH POWDERED SUGAR. *LEKKER!*

November and December are special months for Dutch children. *Sinterklaas* (Saint Nicholas) and his helpers, the *Pieten*, visit the Netherlands bringing chocolate letters, spiced cookies, and gifts to all kids.

is for PLAYGROUNDS
(in Dutch: *speeltuinen*)

AMSTERDAM HAS HUNDREDS OF PLAYGROUNDS—IN PARKS, SQUARES, AND AT NEIGHBORHOOD CORNERS. IN THE CITY YOU CAN ALSO FIND PETTING ZOOS (*KINDERBOERDERIJEN*) AND PADDLING POOLS (*PIERENBADJES*)!

Did you know that metal climbing domes were invented in Amsterdam?

Paddling pool *(pierenbadje)*
Kids love splashing around in a paddling pool on Amsterdam's hot summer days.

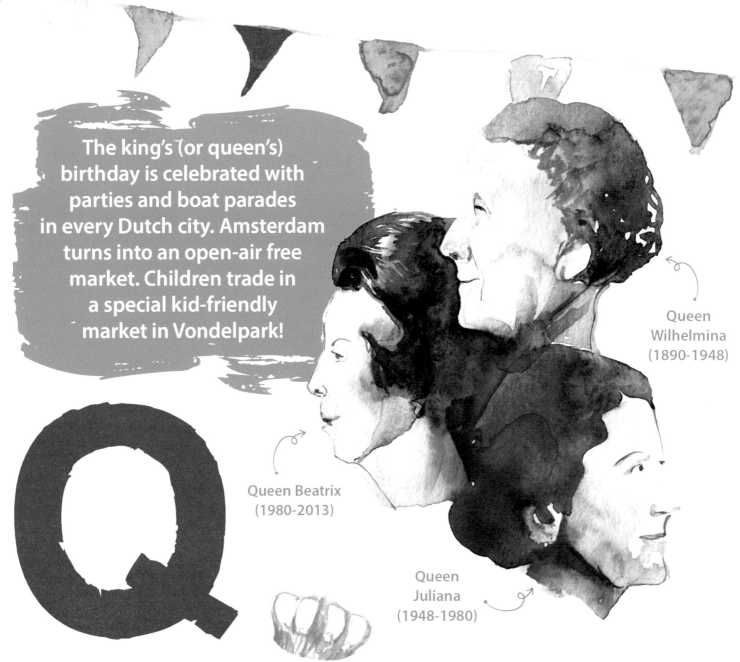

The king's (or queen's) birthday is celebrated with parties and boat parades in every Dutch city. Amsterdam turns into an open-air free market. Children trade in a special kid-friendly market in Vondelpark!

Queen Wilhelmina (1890-1948)

Queen Beatrix (1980-2013)

Queen Juliana (1948-1980)

Q

is for QUEENS
(in Dutch: *koninginnen*)

BEFORE KING WILLEM-ALEXANDER, THE DUTCH THRONE WAS HELD BY QUEENS FOR MORE THAN 120 YEARS.

R

is for
REMBRANDT
VAN RIJN
(1606-1669)

REMBRANDT WAS A PAINTER WHO LIVED IN AMSTERDAM OVER 400 YEARS AGO. HE QUICKLY BECAME A FAMOUS ARTIST, AND PAINTED MANY PORTRAITS, INCLUDING OVER 100 "SELFIES".

Rembrandt painted a group portrait named *Nachtwacht* (Night Watch), one of the most famous Dutch masterpieces.

S is for SKATING
(in Dutch: *schaatsen*)

Skating is very popular in the Netherlands. But, the most popular sport is *voetbal* (football/ soccer). Amsterdam's team AJAX is one of the best in the country!

DURING WINTER, PEOPLE GO ICE SKATING AT THE MANY RINKS THROUGHOUT AMSTERDAM, OR, IF IT GETS COLD ENOUGH, ON THE CANALS. DUTCH KIDS LEARN TO ICE SKATE HOLDING ON TO CHAIRS!

Did you know that tulips originally come from the Himalayas? In time, they were imported to Turkey, and from there to the Netherlands about 500 years ago. Since then, the Netherlands has been the largest producer of tulips in the world!

EVERY JANUARY, THE NETHERLANDS CELEBRATES NATIONAL TULIP DAY. ON THIS DAY, A COLORFUL GARDEN IS SET UP IN THE CITY CENTER WHERE EVERYONE CAN PICK THE VERY FIRST TULIPS OF THE SEASON. LATER ON, BETWEEN APRIL AND MAY, MILLIONS OF TULIPS OF ALL COLORS MAKE AMSTERDAM EVEN MORE BEAUTIFUL!

T is for TULIPS
(in Dutch: *tulpen*)

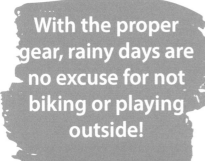

With the proper gear, rainy days are no excuse for not biking or playing outside!

U

is for
UMBRELLA
(in Dutch: *paraplu*)

Waterproof jacket

Rain boots

Waterproof pants

DUTCH INVENTORS CREATED THE *STORMPARAPLU* (STORM UMBRELLA), AN UNUSUALLY-SHAPED UMBRELLA THAT WON'T FLIP INSIDE OUT ON AMSTERDAM'S FREQUENT WINDY AND RAINY DAYS.

is for
VINCENT VAN GOGH
(1853-1890)

WORLD-FAMOUS DUTCH PAINTER VAN GOGH
LIVED IN AMSTERDAM ONLY BRIEFLY. BUT
HERE YOU CAN SEE MOST OF HIS ART IN
A MUSEUM NAMED AFTER HIM.

The way the Dutch pronounce
the letter "g" is unique.
It takes non-native speakers
a lot of practice to master it!

When Van Gogh moved to France,
he started to sign his art with his first name
because people there found it hard
to pronounce his last name.

THERE ARE OVER 1,000 WINDMILLS IN THE NETHERLANDS, SOME OF WHICH ARE STILL ACTIVE. THEY MOSTLY POWER MILLSTONES TO MAKE FLOUR, BUT SOME ARE STILL USED TO PUMP WATER TO KEEP THE SURROUNDING LAND DRY.

In the past, there were dozens of windmills just in Amsterdam. Only eight of these marvelous machines are still standing today.

W
is for WINDMILL
(in Dutch: *windmolen*)

This is the *Riekermolen.*

THREE WHITE CROSSES ON A RED SHIELD WITH A BLACK BAND ARE THE SYMBOL OF THE CITY OF AMSTERDAM.

X

is for XXX

The three crosses can be seen on flags, buildings, and even t-shirts. The most unique place to find them are short posts that divide streets and sidewalks, affectionately called *Amsterdammertjes* (little Amsterdammers).

Y

is for YACHT

Over 1,500 English words are actually Dutch words, just spelled differently! Do you recognize these words?

koekjes • • waffle
schaats • • spooky
pinkje • • pinky
wafel • • cookies
spook • • skate

YACHT COMES FROM THE DUTCH WORD *JACHT*, A LIGHT, FAST BOAT USED TO CHASE PIRATES ALONG THE DUTCH COASTLINE CENTURIES AGO.

is for
TOT ZIENS
(formal Dutch word for See you later!)

NOW YOU KNOW THE ABCs OF AMSTERDAM, AND YOU ARE READY TO
GO EXPLORE. *VEEL PLEZIER* (HAVE FUN) DISCOVERING THIS
BEAUTIFUL CITY, AND *TOT ZIENS!*

MAP OF AMSTERDAM

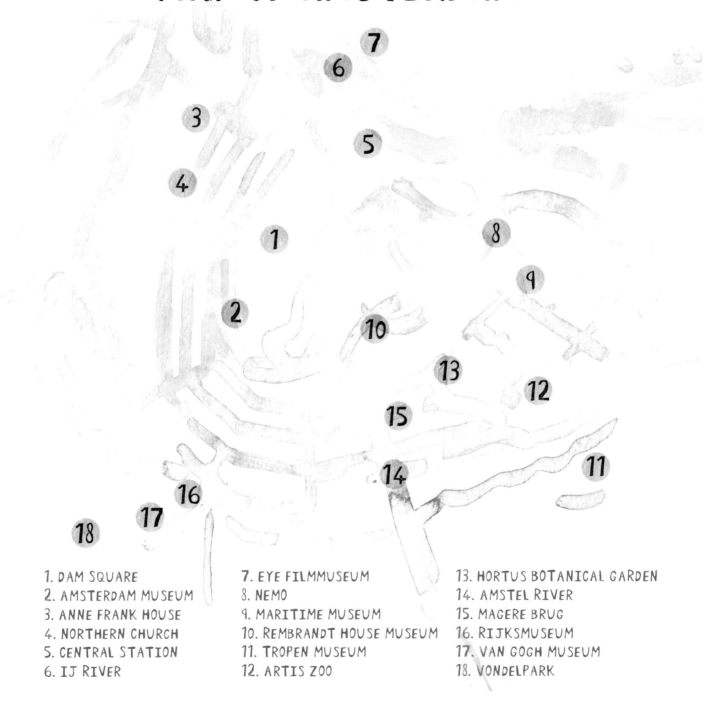

1. DAM SQUARE
2. AMSTERDAM MUSEUM
3. ANNE FRANK HOUSE
4. NORTHERN CHURCH
5. CENTRAL STATION
6. IJ RIVER

7. EYE FILMMUSEUM
8. NEMO
9. MARITIME MUSEUM
10. REMBRANDT HOUSE MUSEUM
11. TROPEN MUSEUM
12. ARTIS ZOO

13. HORTUS BOTANICAL GARDEN
14. AMSTEL RIVER
15. MAGERE BRUG
16. RIJKSMUSEUM
17. VAN GOGH MUSEUM
18. VONDELPARK

TWELVE DUTCH WORDS TO KNOW

Hoi/Hallo	*(hoy/ hal-loh)*	Hello
Daag	*(dahkh)*	**Goodbye**
Doei (doei)	*(doee (doee))*	**Bye (bye)**
Tot ziens	*(toht zeens)*	See you soon!
Goedemorgen	*(khoo-duh-mawr-ghuh)*	Good Morning!
Dankjewel	*(dahnk-yuh-vehl)*	**Thank you**
Graag gedaan	*(khrahkh khuh-dahn)*	**You're welcome**
Alsjeblieft	*(ahl-shuh-bleeft)*	Please
Pardon	*(pahr-dohn)*	Excuse me!
Sorry	*(saw-ree)*	**I'm sorry**
Ja	*(yah)*	**Yes**
Nee	*(nay)*	No

MEMORIES AND NOTES

Draw your favorite Amsterdam memory!

Made in the USA
Columbia, SC
12 March 2024

33016316R00020